God's Beauty Queens

21 Days of True Beauty Empowerment

God's Beauty Queens

21 Days of True Beauty Empowerment

MASLANDE "MandyFresh FREDERIC

God's Beauty Queens: 21 Days of True Beauty Empowerment

Copyright © 2017 – Mandy Frederic

ISBN: 978-0-692-96885-7

Published by: Faces Made Beautiful LLC

Book Cover Design: Tia Cooke of Cooke Consulting & Creations LLC

Printed in the United States of America.- First Edition

Contents

Acknowledgments

I would like to take the time to thank the Lord Jesus Christ for giving me an opportunity to share his words of inspiration. I also would like to thank my pastors, church sisters, and community for supporting the vision that God has placed in me.

I also would like to thank my team, which are my sisters, Merline Joseph, Ernide Frederic, and Adleine Frederic. I love you guys so much; you inspire me to be great and reach for the galaxies. I also would like to thank my mother, Merelie Frederic, and father, Thelusma Frederic, for always being there and encouraging me to be great.

Mandy Fresh Frederic

Foreword

When I was asked to write the foreword for this book, I must admit that I was both honored and terrified. Writing a foreword for the first time was challenging enough, but being asked to credit a book written to minister to women, I thought was kind of out of my realm.

However, as I read this book, I couldn't help but to be enamored by the heartfelt spiritual affirmations and transparency that Mandy Frederic brings to this beautifully crafted work. In a world filled with superficial expressions of beauty, the author meticulously identifies the true essence of the inner beauty that God has created in every individual.

For many women, makeup has become the tool that hides the deep wounds and pain of rejection, abuse, depression, and low self-esteem. But as the concealer begins to fade, they discover that their desire for self-actualization cannot be merely brushed on and wiped off, as it must be discovered from within. This book is a roadmap that will lead you to discovering the true essence of the beauty that God has created within you. The daily affirmations are the road markers to remind you to keep moving forward as you endeavor to unlock the doors to your inner greatness.

As her bishop for the past five years, I've had the privilege and joy to experience Mandy Frederic grow through the stages of healing in her own life. I've watched the shackles of her insecurities fall from her hands as she reached out to become a mentor to women in the community. To simply say that I'm honored to write this foreword would understate the enthusiasm and pleasure that I have after reading this book.

Bishop D.G. Hood
Bishop, The Enrichment Center, Fort Lauderdale, Florida

Introduction

Hello Beauty Queen! If you're reading this first line, then you are on the journey to discovering your true beauty from within. Know that you have invested in a bright and beautiful future. I am your True Beauty Coach, MandyFresh Frederic, here to guide you and show you what true beauty really is. We live in a world full of shallowness and superficiality, where people are praised based on appearance and not character. But what is true beauty? Is it the amount of makeup, clothes, shoes, or any material goods that one has? No! I have found that beauty has to be much deeper than that.

As a little girl growing up in sunny South Florida, I always had a need in my soul to be wanted and validated by people. No matter what I did, I always tried my best to fit in the crowd. I thought that kids could be so mean. I never understood what true beauty was. I always knew that God had his hand on my life, but that still wasn't enough to fill up the emptiness I felt inside as a young girl. Many would assume that I didn't grow up with a father figure to validate me, but I did.

I became very self-conscious about my complexion and weight. Some told me I wasn't pretty enough, light enough, or small enough. All of this opened the door to low self-esteem. I became so disgusted with myself. So, again I ask, what is true beauty? I am reminded of a scripture in the Bible by King David in Psalm 139:14 that says, "I will praise thee; for I am fearfully and wonderfully made: marvellous are thy works; and that my soul knoweth right well." We are fearfully and wonderfully made by God, and he doesn't make mistakes. We were formed and created by the master of beauty himself. We were created with such eloquence and uniqueness in the image of God. We are his greatest expression of love. There were seasons in my life where I didn't understand the love of God. But, when I encountered God's love, I then realized his love is true beauty. The enemy had me believing a lie.

As women in this society, we have been painted a false image about being beautiful. I have battled for quite some time with low self-esteem issues, always questioning how people see me. So, my focus was always on the outer appearance. Don't get me wrong, there is nothing wrong with wanting to look beautiful and being healthy. What I am addressing is this false sense of beauty the world is so dogmatic about promoting, that is solely based on outer appearance instead of the gift of wholeness that radiates through the soul; that is true beauty. True beauty can only be obtained once it has been embedded on the inside.

Most of us struggle with accepting who we are, because someone told you a lie and you believed it. Just like me, you may have been told you that you weren't pretty enough, small enough, or not light enough. If so, this book will take you on a journey that will help build your self-confidence by discovering you beauty from within. God has given me twenty-one days of nuggets that really transitioned my life from one place to the next. This book is written in simplicity. As you commit the next twenty-one days to reading this book, your life will never be the same. I am challenging you to be committed and take this life-changing journey, where you will be able to see yourself the way God sees you. Take the time to reflect where you are right now and know that this book will help transform your mind on how you view yourself. It will also help build self-confidence and boost your self-esteem.

God's
Beauty Queens

Day One
Your Mindset is the Key Attribute that Exudes True Beauty from the Inside

Have you ever been around someone who is always negative about everything? Do you realize that negative behavior is adaptable? There's a proverbial saying that I always hear people say: birds of a feather flock together. In other words, you are who you acquaint yourself with. I also love what the Bible says in Proverbs 22:24-25 (NIV): "Do not make friends with a hot-tempered person, do not associate with one easily angered, or you may learn their ways and get yourself ensnared." If you hang around a hot-tempered person, I can guarantee you'll pick up habits that you never had before. You must be very careful of your surroundings. People can influence the way you think, good or bad. You must separate yourself from all negative influences or they will overtake you. What you must realize is that who you allow around you and tolerate, will eventually have an effect on you.

Ladies, what is your thought process? What do you allow to take center stage in your mind? You have to also be mindful of what you entertain in your mind. There was a season of my life where I couldn't quite get a grip on my thoughts. I allowed negative imaginations to become a playground in my mind. This caused me to respond to things in an extremely negative manner. How did I know that? I could never see the good in anything; my responses to spontaneous situations were always negative. Negativity will plague your mind so bad, it starts to mess with yourself self-esteem. You must also understand your mind is the gateway to every action you make. In other words, your emotions will dictate how you feel about yourself then produce actions! It can be good actions or self-sabotaging.

Do a self-evaluation, analyze your surroundings, and assess where is the problem. Allow God to show you where you need to be mended. I'm reminded of the scripture in Romans 12:2 that speaks about being transformed by the renewing of your mind! In other words, you are what you set your mind on, and that is what will become your reality. For example, if you see yourself as worthless, you will remain worthless. As your beauty coach for the rest of this journey, I challenge you to reprogram your mind. Begin to speak positively over your life using the Word of God. Begin to declare how beautiful you are. God has created you fearfully and wonderful in his sight. You are beautiful and there is nothing anyone can do about it.

Your Thoughts _____

_____

_____

_____

_____

_____

_____

_____

_____

_____

_____

_____

_____

Today's Affirmation

I have a beautiful mind and beauty resides within me.

Day Two
True Inner Beauty Reflects Wholeness in the Soul

What brings true fulfillment to you? Have you ever asked yourselves that question? Many times, as women, we use external pleasures to fill empty spaces. Ladies, let's do a reality check; people, places, or things cannot and will not bring true fulfillment or happiness. Total wholeness must come from a source outside of material things. Where do you place your worth? Is your worth based on how many friends you have or, better yet, how people make you feel good about yourself? If so, there is a huge problem. Even though this is prominent in today's society, we must not give in to what we see.

Have you ever been shopping with your girlfriends and you see an outfit that you *really* like? You ask your girlfriends for their opinion and they say they don't like it. You fell in love with the outfit the moment you laid your eyes on it. But as soon as you received a second opinion that didn't agree with yours, your mind shifted. This only happens when there's no true fulfillment internally. So, what we do is seek validation from the opinion of others in order to feel good about who we are. Others' opinions shouldn't be centered on decisions of your worth. I want you to ponder on that for a while.

How do we tackle and overcome internal insecurities and feelings of emptiness? The only way to overcome internal emptiness is through the love of God. Do you have a spiritual connection with your heavenly Father? True fulfillment only comes from the love of God and being in the beauty of his presence! There's a place in God that our souls long for! There a scripture that most of us are familiar, Psalm 23:1 which says, "The Lord is my shepherd; I shall not want." In other words, whatever your internal need is, it can be found in the Lord! God's presence and his Word will unlock everything that you need. In his presence there is fullness of joy. Everything that you thought you needed to fulfill you will be a thing in the past.

I want you to make a conscious decision to make God's Word and presence a priority in your life. I am telling you from experience that once you have an encounter with the agape love and Word of God, you will never be the same. I speak total fulfillment in you now. I declare that your life is changing for the better *now*. You will not want for anything; the love of God is finding you right now. May every broken place be rebuilt by the love of God in Jesus' name. RECEIVE IT.

Your Thoughts _____

_____

_____

_____

_____

_____

_____

_____

_____

_____

_____

_____

_____

Today's Affirmation
*There's nothing in me missing nor broken. I live in total
fulfillment through the beauty of God's holiness.*

Day Three

In a place Called Adversity, True Beauty is Birthed

Adversity can sometimes come when you least expect it. So, what do we do when faced with life challenges? We can choose to throw in the towel or fight. Ladies, you must look at the positive side to every bad situation. Don't allow adversity or circumstance cause you to lose hope. There will be seasons in your life where things will not go exactly how you plan; it causes frustration, but I believe in every circumstance God has a plan. You should know and understand that adversity only comes to build you and make you stronger. It builds you from the inside out, if you let it. You can't take on a posture of defeat, for in the midst of every situation, there is a hidden blessing. Life can happen to anybody; it's how you handle it that determines the level of victory that you walk out. Pressure comes to bring out the best in you, if you allow it. God has given you power to overcome any adversity that comes your way.

Let's use the analogy of a diamond. We understand that before a diamond has value, it must first be dug from the ground. Once the diamond is discovered, it's covered in dirt. The diamond must go through a various pressure before it becomes valuable. Just like a diamond, there may be seasons in your life where you feel like you are in the dirt and there is pressure on every side. But remember that after the dirt is removed and the pressure ceases, you have something very valuable.

I remember at my former job there was an incident that occurred at work. I didn't have anything to do with the issue, but the supervisor decided that she was going to take out her frustration on me. I didn't like the way she addressed me. She became abrupt in conversation. The way she spoke to me made me feel extremely uncomfortable. I was the type of person that always felt I had to defend myself. What I did not realize was that God wanted to heal me from that offense and my attitude about it. God was molding me, teaching me how not to take things to heart, and to freely forgive. God doesn't want us defending ourselves; he wants to fight our battles for us. Second Chronicles 20 speaks of a king named Jehoshaphat. He was faced with a circumstance where it seemed he could not win. The Word of the Lord came to him telling him be not dismayed or afraid for the battle is the Lord's not his. So, there are times when God will allow circumstances to arise to show you who he is. In the same way, God used that situation at my job to build my character.

What are you facing that seems to be challenging? Whatever it is trust God enough to know that he's working it out for your good. I challenge you to change the way you perceive adversity. Adversity can only build you and make you stronger. God has given you the power to overcome all things that come your way! Beauty Queens, I want you to know whatever you're going through, God can handle it. Don't allow adversity or the cares of this world to get you off track. Adversity only comes for a season. This, too, shall pass--whatever it is you're dealing with. I speak into your life: you are moving forward. Every heavy weight that would come to try and hold you bound, know that God hasn't given you more than you can handle. God has you in the palm of his hand. You are royalty.

Your Thoughts _____

_____

_____

_____

_____

_____

_____

_____

_____

_____

_____

_____

Today's Affirmation
I am an overcomer and beauty lives within me.

Day Four
True Inner Beauty is Not Based on the Conditions Around You

Beauty Queens, I want you to ask yourself a question: Am I living or just surviving? What conditions are you attracting into your life? God has empowered you with an ability to influence the environment surrounding your life. You have the ability to speak a thing into existence. There are many of you living in a condition that God hasn't ordained for you. What you don't realize is that you create the condition with what you think and speak. What am I saying? Some of us tend to speak whatever comes to our mind without any reserve and then we wonder why nothing seems to be working out in our life. Have you considered that the words you speak may be the reason why your life isn't going the way you want it. We are speaking spirits, and what you speak out of your mouth is alive. Remember God created us in his image and likeness. Everything that God created he spoke it into existence. What am I saying? The conditions around your life are not by accident or happenstance. We create our conditions with the words that we speak. The words we speak cause us to bear good or bad fruits.

What happens when different situations arise in your life? Are you moving by what you see? God has given us the power to speak to our circumstances. You have to program your mind to be mentally conscious to respond when different circumstances pop up in your life. You have to speak the opposite of what you see because your words have the ability to change your circumstances. We have been given divine power to speak the Word of God. Your speaking language must shift in order for your conditions to change.

Once we begin to shift our speech, the abundance of life that God has intended for you will begin to manifest. Proverbs 18:21(NLT) says, "The tongue can bring death or life; those who love to talk will reap the consequences." Ladies, let's be mindful of what we allow to come out of our mouths for you shall have what you say! I want you to take a moment and examine what's in your life that's out of alignment. I want you to begin to say these things. Ready? "Everything that's out of alignment in my life come into proper alignment now, in Jesus' name. I declare everything that God has ordained to take place in my life is chasing me down now." Began to inhale and exhale and say out loud, "My life is lining up with the divine will of God for my life." Ladies, I want you to know that you are more than a conqueror, you are strong, and you have the power within you. Receive the strength of God now.

Your Thoughts _____

_____

_____

_____

_____

_____

_____

_____

_____

_____

_____

_____

Today's Affirmation
I am no longer bound by negativity;
I produce a beautiful lifestyle.

Day Five
There is Beauty in the Process of Time

Ladies, beauty is an ongoing process of growth that takes time to build. Being patient during the process produces growth. Inner beauty is continual; it's not something that can be mastered in one shot. Inner beauty takes time; it takes being persistent knowing that there is greater in you that lies within. Have you ever prayed for something or a circumstance that you wanted to change in your life, but it didn't happen as fast as you may have wanted it to? Sometimes in this journey called life, God will allow certain things to remain around to prune and mature you. There will be seasons of uncertainty, but know that God has you right where he wants you.

Sometimes we look at people's lives and think they have it all together. In reality, we just know how to mask it well as women. There is no such thing as perfect people, but we have the gift of masking the truth. However, God never called you to criticize yourself, but to embrace you—all of you, even what you deem flaws. We must learn how not to focus on what we don't like about ourselves by magnifying our uniqueness rather than our flaws. What are you doing to embrace who you are? I know as women there are things that we can work on to improve ourselves. For example, if you're someone who doesn't find pleasure being around other people, work on your people skills. Learn to embrace others outside your environment, race, or culture. It will give you a different perspective about others. In doing that you'll still remain true to who you are. God has fearfully designed you before this time began.

Now, it's time to embrace your flaws, differences, and love on yourself. The only way you're going to truly be able to love yourself is by first finding the love of God. You won't be able to give out what you don't first possess. God has given us the command to love our neighbor as we love ourselves. In order to love, we must encounter the love of God. God is the creator of love. Once we learn the love language of God, we can extend that to someone else because we have experienced it for ourselves. I challenge you to look yourself in the mirror and see the beauty that God has created. You are a work of art. I speak in to your life, ladies, that you will look at yourself differently. May the love of God exude from your life. May you find happiness with embracing who God has created you to be!

Your Thoughts _____

_____

_____

_____

_____

_____

_____

_____

_____

_____

_____

_____

_____

_____

Today's Affirmation

God has created me in the beauty of his majesty.

Day Six

True Inner Beauty Lies in the Willingness to Be Alone in the Process of Becoming Great

Do you know what it takes to truly tap into the grace God has placed on the inside of you? Do you understand the cost? There will be seasons in your life where God will call you to walk alone. It's in that season, you'll be able tap into the resources God has placed on the inside of you. People may not understand your process, but there is a purpose for everything that occurs in your life. Time alone allows you to hear God clearer and receive greater direction concerning your purpose in life. To many times we tend to get distracted with the cares and worries of this life. So many of you have lost sight on what's really important. There will be times when God gets you to a place where you are by yourself in order to get your attention.

I had to go through a process like this as well. I remember it so clearly! God would try to get my attention on certain things, but I was too busy doing nothing. Guess what God had to do? He stripped me from what I thought was a good thing that was actually a distraction. I had to learn the hard way that's not where God wanted me at that particular moment. Now, in the beginning I didn't submit to the process; it took time. I didn't realize that God was making me at the time. I would try to run away from it by doing things prematurely. But it's in the process that greatness is birthed. God doesn't want you to be blessed half way; he wants to give you the whole blessing.

Ladies, there is a process that you must endure. Nothing great ever happens overnight. I want to challenge you to take this moment and evaluate your life. Stop trying to fight the process. It's in the process you'll find great reward. There was a saying my bishop used to always say: you don't go to sleep a blunder and wakeup a wonder. In other words, greatness takes time to create. One must be willing to go through that place of aloneness for a season. It's in those times you discover who you really are. I want you to know that you will make it. Endure the process; you have greatness inside of you. There is beauty that is waiting to be revealed. You're going to make it. You have purpose on the inside of you, just endure the process. I speak assurance into your life; you are not alone. God is with you and you're going to make it.

Your Thoughts _____

_____

_____

_____

_____

_____

_____

_____

_____

_____

_____

_____

Today's Affirmation
I'm living with beauty on the inside of me that shall give birth to purpose.

Day Seven
True Inner Beauty Will Produce Endurance in a Dry Place

Queens, there will be seasons of dryness in your life that will come, but don't be frustrated; it's making you into the woman that God has called you to be. Many times, we frustrate ourselves because we want to figure out every detail that occurs in various periods of our lives. You're not going to understand what's going on, but trust God in the midst of the process. There have been many occasions in my life where I felt frustrated about where I was in life, particularly at the age of 25. There was so many things that I wanted to see happen in my life at that time that didn't occur. I couldn't understand. I wanted to be married with kids already, living a happily ever after. But God had a bigger plan. Sometimes we don't understand his plan at the time; but trust it's for the best.

There was so many internal issues that I had in me that wasn't dealt with. Could you imagine if I was married, where would I be? I do, and I would probably be divorced! I thank God for the process. It was in those dry places that God revealed to me where I was internally. I was so broken and had an identity crisis. I didn't know who I was in God. I thought being married would solve it. Not so! I didn't understand my worth as a woman. I would settle for less on everything! Why? I had low self-esteem.

It was very hard for me to see myself the way God saw me. I only felt good when just about anybody would want to talk to me, gave me self-worth, or validation. But thank God! He loved me so much that he didn't allow marriage in my life or relationship. The dry place was necessary for me to birth what God has placed on the inside of me. I couldn't understand at the time, but God was making me into the woman that I am today.

"Many are the plans in a person's heart, but it is the Lord's purpose that prevails" (Proverbs 19:21 NIV). In other words, we make different plans, things we would like to accomplish at a certain age, time, or year, but we have to understand God's plans are always greater than are plans, so we must trust the process. You may not understand everrything that occurs in our life, but trust and know that it's making you. Understand that dry seasons in your life come to build you and make you stronger. Obstacles come to build, teach, and mature you. Ladies, posture yourself and submit to the process. You shall be great and successful in all that you do. You were created for greatness and purpose lives on the inside of you. Embrace your dry seasons and go forth.

Your Thoughts _____

_____

_____

_____

_____

_____

_____

_____

_____

_____

_____

_____

_____

Today's Affirmation

I will endure the process and reap a harvest.

Beauty Nugget

"Enduring the Process for the Shift"

I am excited that you have challenged yourself to get this far in your journey. In today's society, we see so many definitions of what defines beauty. As you continue to read this book you will receive confidence to be who you were meant to be. I want you to take a moment and begin to ponder on what you want to see take place in your life. The first step to any major shift in your mind, you must first examine your inner most self. Pay attention to your thoughts, your actions, and what you allow to take residence in your mind. Your thoughts will create patterns about how you see yourself. Negative thoughts will always influence the way you see yourself. Be mindful of your thoughts, ladies! Are ready for the shift? You must prepare themselves mentally for a transition.

In transition, there will be bad habits that you must be willing to let go of in order to get the best. Whether it be friendships, relationships, places, or anything else that is keeping you from your very best, God wants to do a new work in you. He wants to fill that emptiness that you feel. You were created with a God-sized hole in you that only God can fill. You must get out of the mindset of needing someone to validate who you already are. You are a beautiful, radiant, bold, daring, and optimistic woman; speak that over your life.

I have realized that beauty is vanity without God. Beauty is not something that can just be placed on with makeup or a nice hair style. It's a character, a charisma about someone's presence that distinguishes them from the rest. As I began this journey of understanding beauty the way God intended, there was a sense of joy that came over me.

The passage in Song of Solomon 4:7 (ESV) says, "You are altogether beautiful, my love; there is no flaw in you." This scripture tells us that we were uniquely fashioned by God. Ladies, there is only one of you. God has designed you for such a time as this. He has created you to do mighty exploits. You must come to a place where you can see the beauty that God has placed on the inside of you. As we continue on this journey I want you to know that you are not alone. Transition isn't always easy, but it is necessary for the next phase of your life. Be encouraged today. Know that each time you wake up in the morning is a new day for you to start working towards your dreams. You are more than where you are currently. God has so much in store for you; he wants to blow your mind with his goodness. It is already done; you have to believe in the process that its working out for your good. It's transition time!

Day Eight
True Inner Beauty Will Cause You to Look Beyond What You See

What do you see when you look around you? Have you ever considered that most of your conditions are based on how you respond? When things that you didn't plan for arise in your life, the determined outcome of that issue or situation will more than likely be determined based on your posture and interpretation of it. Many of us miss the opportunity to learn from life's issues or problems that come our way. True beauty will cause you to see the wisdom in any circumstance. Chapters of your life are being written every day with endless possibilities. What's around you is subject to change at any given moment. You can choose to stay where you are and dwell on past experiences or you can choose to look deeper. God has called you to look beyond what you see. Sometimes your environment doesn't mirror what God has planned for you, but there is so much greater for you. I want you to receive that internally.

God has given you a mind to imagine and think beyond what you see. Imagination is a powerful tool that God has given you. It gives you the image of the goals that you would like to fulfill. I remember years ago imagining myself writing a book about beauty that would speak to women from all walks of life. I would even picture the book cover. Although my environment at the time did not mirror what God had placed on the inside of me, I never gave into what I saw because I felt that there was greater in store for me. I saw myself writing a book that would touch many women. Now here I am! I'm challenging you to look beyond what you see and step out of your limitations. Dare to think bigger and dream out loud. What are your dreams? What do you see yourself doing?

Some of us today are unsure of how to step out on faith. I am challenging you to move beyond your limitations. Don't focus on what you don't have. Acknowledge God in everything that you're doing, and he shall direct your path. You must learn to trust God, with all that you have. I want you to stay focused on the bigger picture. God is calling you to succeed in every aspect of your life, Beauty Queens. Remember, imagination is powerful tool, so use it. This week set aside some time to meditate. It's in the time of mediation that you'll receive direction on how to fulfill your dreams or goals.

Your Thoughts _____

_____

_____

_____

_____

_____

_____

_____

_____

_____

_____

_____

Today's Affirmation
I will succeed, and failure is not an option.

Day Nine
True Inner Beauty is Cause for Celebration

Today, ladies, I want you to know that I celebrate you! Beauty is all about celebration and acknowledgment of God's perfection in the earth. You were formed and fashioned with perfection. Everything about you was made perfect with God's ingredients. There is only one of you in this entire world. God has placed his unique DNA in you that no one can duplicate. Celebrate your differences and embrace them. What I notice among some women is that we spend most of time comparing ourselves to the next person. We compare our looks, height, color, weight, and shape. And that comes from lack of contentment and fulfillment with who you are.

Lack of fulfillment will cause you to hide behind material possessions, careers, friends, and status. God never intended it this way. He sent his Son Jesus so that you can have life and have it more abundantly. There is nothing wrong with success; it only becomes a problem when your identity is based on what you can or have achieved. So, today, I want you to celebrate yourself. Learn to be content with your identity, whether you're short or tall, skinny or fat, light skin or dark skin—you are beautiful. Take a mirror and look at yourself. Begin to say, "I am beautiful, bold, confident, and courageous." Everything that you will ever need is on the inside of you.

Your Thoughts _____

_____

_____

_____

_____

_____

_____

_____

_____

_____

_____

_____

_____

Today's Affirmation
I am more than a conqueror.

Day Ten
True Inner Beauty Gives You the Boldness and Tenacity to Stand Out from the Norm

Ladies, has there ever been a time in your life that you wanted to step out and do something that wasn't quite common? In other words, doing something that's hasn't been done before. Today, it seems that no one is willing to step outside of their comfort zone, preferring instead to be people pleasers. We don't want to offend anyone with our God-given creativity because everyone wants to play it safe. Ladies, God hasn't called you to play it safe; he has placed the beauty of creativity that will propel you to the next phase of your life, if you're willing to take a chance. I remember seasons ago, I didn't have the confidence to step out and be different. I was too busy trying to fit in. But God never called me to fit in; he called me to blaze trails!

Let's begin to stand out from the crowd. No longer will you play it safe due to others' opinions. I challenge you to step outside the box. What is it that you have wanted to do for a long time that you never had the courage to do? Writing this book to encourage you Beauty Queens wasn't easy for me. I had to get over my fear of whether or not people would accept it. What we must realize is that when God gives you a vision, it may not seem normal at first. To some people it will not make sense, and some may have a problem with it. Guess what? It doesn't matter what they think. I had to get to a place in my mind of accepting who I was and being okay with it. It's okay to be different; you don't have to follow the status quo. Whatever dreams you set your mind to do, know that God is with you. Philippians 4:13 reminds you that you can do all things through Christ Jesus that strengthens you.

Your Thoughts _____

_____

_____

_____

_____

_____

_____

_____

_____

_____

Today's Affirmation
I accept who I am and celebrate my differences.

Day Eleven
True Inner Beauty Gives You the Grace to Come Out Victorious

Ladies, there will be times in your life that challenges will seem as if they are coming to wear you out. I have learned to embrace life challenges! Challenges give you a better scope on how you view different situations. We must understand challenges don't come to kill us but to make us better. I remember times when I couldn't articulate the things that was happening around me. I started to feel a little defeated. What I didn't realize was God allowed certain trials in my life to get my attention. What am I trying to convey here? True inner beauty is usually birthed during the most trying times. It is a process that God allows you to face to prune and establish you as queens.

I am reminded of Jeremiah 29:11 (NIV) that says, "For I know the plans I have for you," declares the Lord, "plans to prosper you and not to harm you, plans to give you hope and a future." God wants you to succeed in everything that you do. Before he allows you to walk in that wealthy place, however, you must first go through that process called life. God isn't out to get you; he's building your character in the process, which will qualify you to handle whatever blessings he brings your way. I am repeating it again: you must properly go through the process in order to be qualified to handle the weight and responsibility that comes with it.

I want you to be reminded that you are loved! As your coach, I commend you for taking this step and submitting to the process. You shall be victorious in all that your do!

Your Thoughts _____

_____

_____

_____

_____

_____

_____

_____

_____

_____

Today's Affirmation

I will accomplish great things, for I was created for more.

Day Twelve
True Inner Beauty is Like a Mirror

Queens, you're created for more! There is so much resilience on the inside of you. You can't be the one to undermine your own abilities to succeed; live a life of abundance. God has created you to live a life that promotes wholeness. To many times we can be our own worst critic when it comes to making life decisions that can make or break us. I had to come to the realization that there were decisions that had to be made in order for me to move forward.

Ask yourself why do you allow people, places, or things to remain in your life longer than it has to. You hold on to things that God is telling you to let go. The reason you do this is because you don't know who you truly are. Holding on things that have expired will only do one thing; it will bring rottenness into your life. Your ability to see God the way he sees you will be undermined. So, I am challenging you to evaluate your life and see what needs to go and who you need to let go of to move forward. Psalms 37:23 (KJV) says, "The steps of a good man are ordered by the LORD: and he delighteth in his way." I know some decisions that you make may be a bit difficult. Some decisions will require you letting go of some people, possibly even giving

45

up familiar but unhealthy habits. Pray and allow God to lead you. Evaluate your life; take this moment to think about areas in your life that need to be improved. Now begin making the necessary changes; it's not going to be easy, but it's worth it!

Your Thoughts _____

_____

_____

_____

_____

_____

_____

_____

_____

_____

_____

_____

Affirmation

I mirror what God has placed on the inside of me.

Day Thirteen
True Inner Beauty is Confident

Queens, we can all attest to being insecure about ourselves at one time or another. Insecurities are present when we really don't know who we are, and fail to embrace the gifting that have been bestowed upon us from our heavenly Father. Insecurities normally have us comparing our self to another or even coveting what that person has. You must come into a full understanding of what you possess on the inside so that you don't covet what another person has.

What is the deep-rooted issue that causes this action? At one point in my life, I used to covet what my friends had. I also wanted to be them, talk like them, and dress like them. I'm sure you get the picture. I didn't appreciate the differences and uniqueness that God had allowed me to walk in. So, guess what happened? I lost my own identity trying to be someone else. I had to go through a serious soul searching with God to get my identity back. I had to relearn how to embrace my differences. It's OK to be different.

What we sometimes fail to understand or forget is that God has created you with something that other people need and vice versa. Can you imagine that if you spent more time discovering your abilities, you would have a less likely chance of neither comparing yourself nor wanting what the next woman possesses? How do we get to that place? It will require you spending quality time with God and examining where you are. Get to know the God-given gifts that has been placed down on the inside of you. Once you work on maximizing your abilities, insecurities will fall to the side, and your inner confidence will emerge like never before. Begin to discover the beauty that God has eloquently graced you with and work it.

Your Thoughts _____

_____

_____

_____

_____

_____

_____

_____

_____

Today's Affirmation
I embrace love my differences and walk confidently in them.

Day Fourteen
True Inner Beauty is Disciplined

Have you ever started a vision or a goal that you just couldn't seem to finish? What's the thing that's been holding you back? Distraction comes in many forms that we are unaware of. These distractions can stop us from moving forward in our destiny. We have to be mindful of what's in our environment. As creatures of habits, we tend to mimic what is around us. If you're around a lot of distractions, it will be very detrimental to the progression of your goals. Sometimes we put off goals because of the inner struggles that we deal with as women.

There have been moments in my life where I couldn't quite understand the reasons for my setbacks. Once I analyzed myself, I came to the conclusion that it was mainly my fears holding me back. I had a fear of failure, rejection, misunderstanding, and lack of confidence. I had to go through the process of knowing who I am, in order to let go those fears go. It wasn't an easy process to overcome, being that I had been functioning in that posture for a while. I had to do some more soul searching. I had to deal with those lingering issues that I was struggling with one by one. I didn't overcome this on my own. I had divine intervention from the heavenly Father. As I allowed God to take me through that process, I began to operate in a level of boldness that I never had before.

We were created to conquer whatever obstacle that comes in our way! I am reminded of scripture in the Bible that says, "For God hath not given us the spirit of fear; but of power, and of love, and of a sound mind" (2 Timothy 1:7 KJV). Ladies, we have to be courageous, disciplined, and focused about the dreams and visions that God has given us. I challenge you to step out in faith, trust God, and watch him bring it to pass. You have the created power to finish what you started. I believe in you.

Your Thoughts _____

_____

_____

_____

_____

_____

_____

_____

_____

_____

Today's Affirmation
I have creative power to accomplish greatness.

Beauty Nugget

"It's Time to Transition, Ladies"

Ladies, I commend you on your commitment to finishing this book. We have seven more days to go. I want to encourage you this is a daily process and it's continual. We must posture ourselves to be determined to discover our beauty from within. I want to remind you that everything that you are in search for is already on the inside of you. God has equipped us with eternal beauty that is never ending. Do you know that you have the power to change your reality? It's simple! Change your mind and your life will follow. We must walk in confidence inspite of what it looks like. How do you do that? Well I'm glad you asked! Everything that you will ever conquer must be first conquered from within. You can't continue to walk in the place of insecurity or doubt; we must know who we are. We are queens in the eyes of our heavenly Father. You need to see your value. Realize that there is only one you; God has carefully put you together.

There may be times you will feel that you are incapable of accomplishing what God has set for you to accomplish. You must push pass what you see and walk it out though faith; by pressing forward, towards the mark of the high calling. God has placed a gift on the inside of you. Do you realize that you have eternal beauty that radiates on the inside of you? It's not by mere feeling or something that is tangible in the natural. This beauty is supernatural; it goes beyond what you can articulate.

You must learn to tap into the resource that God has placed on the inside of you. God downloads daily benefits on the inside of us, while renewing his grace. How are we going to do that? We must get rid of obscurity, doubt, and insecurities. The only way to do that will be through the love of God. Once we discover the love of God, we can tap into the beauty. The Bible states in Genesis 1:27 that we're created in the image of God and his likeness. God has an everlasting love that he has made available to us through his Son, Jesus Christ. For God so loved the world that he would give up something so valuable and precious. Ladies, you are precious in the eyes of God. God loves you. You must start to see yourself as beauty queens. Don't settle. God didn't settle, He gave us his best, and that was through his Son, Jesus Christ. We have been given access to this eternal love. As you continue this journey, I want to encourage you to allow the process of this time in your life to take full course. Queens, it is worth it!

Day Fifteen
True Inner Beauty is a Light that Cannot Be Hidden

As beauty queens, do you realize that you have a light that radiates from the inside of you that cannot be hidden? You have greatness that cannot be hidden. God has endowed his beauty on you. What are you doing with this greatness? Are you allowing the cares of this world to distract you? As women, we can't allow distractions or the cares of this world to prohibit us from moving forward and tapping into true greatness.

During this process of writing this book, there were many distractions. Lack of resources was one, which produced a lack of faith for funds to birth out this book. I had to realize my negative thoughts weren't of God; I was walking in fear. Quickly I got a grip of the negative state of mind that I was in because it was hindering me from producing this book. The Bible states in Proverbs 4:25 (MSG): "Keep your eyes straight ahead; ignore all sideshow distractions." If you apply this healthy habit, such as evaluating negative "thoughts" that enter your mind, you'll able to quickly reject anything that comes as a distraction. In doing this, you'll be able to unleash your greatness.

I speak into your lives, ladies, you are a treasure in this earth that cannot be hidden. God has placed a lamp on the inside of you and the world is waiting on you to shine. You were created with so much greatness there is no way you can fail with God on your side. You were created with the gift of creativity. God formed you before this world even began. There was a need for you and that's why you're here. I want you to believe that, because it's true.

Your Thoughts _____

_____

_____

_____

_____

_____

_____

_____

_____

_____

Today's Affirmation
I walk with light and shine everywhere I go.

Day Sixteen
True Inner Beauty Illuminates

Have you ever been in a place of confusion? Or have you ever felt hopeless and couldn't quite understand what was going on around you? It just felt like one thing after another, right? It's in those moments that you should seek God for clarity. I, too, have been in those seasons in my life. Can you imagine being born into a community and having to transition after twenty-five years? I remember like it just happened. I had to leave my church community of worship and fellowship because God was calling me elsewhere. In the midst of my transition, I was confused, had no sense of direction, or understanding of why would God direct me to leave. I was born there!

But it was in that moment that I had to get in a silent place where I could hear from God. Meditation is what got me through those times of uncertainties. I am here to tell you God wants to turn your uncertainties around. Get in a place of meditation with the Lord. It's in those places clarity and understanding will be produced. God wants you to be healthy, wealthy, and wise. God never wants his daughters to be in a state of blindness, where you can't quite comprehend what's going on around you. I reminded of Psalm 32:8 (KJV): "I will instruct thee and teach thee in the way which thou shalt go: I will guide thee with mine eye." I believe when we get to that place of meditation, God will give us illuminating clarity.

Your Thoughts _____

_____

_____

_____

_____

_____

_____

_____

_____

_____

_____

Today's Affirmation
I am a child of the king; I renounce confusion from over
my life in Jesus' name.

Day Seventeen
True Inner Beauty is Discovered Through Pressure

Every elevation that occurs in one's life is obtained through a process of pressure. Have you ever looked at a situation or event that took place in your life but didn't quite understand it? I have been in a place of process in my life time and questioned why is this happening to me, instead of me observing the situation to find out what am I to learn from this. For example, I remember during my time of employment searches, I expected that with my background and education, I should have landed a successful career already. That process was challenging for me because I didn't recognize that God allowed me to go through that process to see myself. Knowing myself, I wanted the door to be open right away for me. However, God had other plans.

Through this process, God was teaching me patience. In the midst of understanding my process, I grew less frustrated and more aware of what God was teaching me at that time. Ladies, you have to understand, good things come through the process of patience. You may have a vision or goal that you want to accomplish, and it's just seems like the process is ongoing or it's not coming together as quickly as you would like. But, I believe if you trust God with it and wait on him, he will open the right doors.

It's in those times that God is producing his character of beauty in you. I'm reminded of James 1:4 (KJV) states, "But let patience have her perfect work, that ye may be perfect and entire, wanting nothing."

Your Thoughts _____

_____

_____

_____

_____

_____

_____

_____

_____

_____

Today's Affirmation
I am destined to win.

Day Eighteen

True Inner Beauty Will Attract Favor and Grace

Queens, I believe strongly in this phrase: your attitude will determine your altitude. How do people view you? Do people see you as being a pleasant person to be acquainted with or do people run away when they see you? Take a moment to reflect on that. As a beauty coach, one exercise I use with women is to help them understand that makeup is just one layer of beauty. Beauty is a presence that people sense when they are around you. Inner beauty will attract favor, grace, and the right people. You can't expect positive people around you if you're negative all the time; they won't stay.

A good attitude will cause you to stretch beyond your thinking. Positive attitude will propel you from one place to the next. Your attitude also controls how you respond in faith. Think about it. If you have dreams and goals that you would like to accomplish, a positive attitude will always propel you in faith to make a move on it. Why? You have already thought that it's going to happen. In doing that, you'll move the heart of God. He'll send the right people to give you favor to produce what you've set your heart out to do. The Bible declares that we are more than conquerors. We must learn to conquer our attitude. Be positive despite what situation may and will arise. Always look at the situation from a positive perspective. Your attitude alone can change your situation for the best or for the worst. No more looking at the glass as half empty. Begin to see it as half full.

Your Thoughts _____

_____

_____

_____

_____

_____

_____

_____

_____

_____

_____

_____

Today's Affirmation
Favor and graces resides in my life.

Day Nineteen
True Inner Beauty Will Cause You to Transition

Beauty Queens, did you know that timeliness is also a determining factor of the outcomes in your life. You must be very diligent with the time that God has placed in your hand. No longer will you misuse time on the wrong things. What do I mean by that? Have you ever been in a relationship that was a waste of time? I want you to evaluate your relationship circle. Let's consider romantic relationships. I have seen many circumstances where we tend to hold onto a relationship that we know is going absolutely nowhere. When it comes to dating, I believe with much prayer and consideration from our heavenly Father, you should know within six months whether the guy you're dating is the one for you. Some may call this women's intuition, but I called it being able to discern. If you have discerned that this relationship is not progressing, don't continue to misuse your time by staying in it.

There are times God shows you the signs that he isn't the one, but you ignore them. You hope one day that your potential will somehow evolve into the man you always dreamed of. I have news for you ladies: he not changing for you! So why are you wasting your time again? There's a quote from Maya Angelou that I love and believe is even more relevant today: *"When someone shows you who they are believe them the first time."* You don't have to waste time trying to figure people out because they will show you.

There's a scripture in the Bible that I am reminded of. To paraphrase, it says that the blessings of the Lord add no sorrows. In other words, God's blessing will always add and not subtract. I want you to evaluate the relationships and friendships that are around you. Stop wasting time with people who don't mean you any good. Make a conscious decision not to waste time in dead relationships that will only hurt you more in the end.

Your Thoughts _____

_____

_____

_____

_____

_____

_____

_____

_____

Today's Affirmation
I am valuable and worth the time.

Day Twenty

True Inner Beauty Will Shift You into Purpose

Why is it important to focus? What motivates you to do what you do? I have come to understand in this journey called life that you must focus on what's important. Have you written some things down to complete within the next few years of your life? What are you planning to accomplish? Have you already started working towards them? I want you to think deeply about the things that you have not accomplished yet. I believe too many times as women, we tend to lose focus on the bigger picture.

I believe distractions come to throw you off your focus. Sometimes when you plan to accomplish a goal you always seem to get side tracked. But, you must train and discipline your mind to be focused. Can you imagine if you were to stay focus on your goals, one day at a time, how far you would be? I remember there was a season in my life where I wanted to lose weight but couldn't quite manage the time to do it. I wrote the plan down and I made my vision plan, but I wasn't focused on it. It just seemed the time I set out for me to exercise, something always came up. Until one day I became frustrated with myself and realized I was allowing distractions to detour me. It may not be exercise for you; it may be your relationship with God, or the business that you have been trying to start for a while.

We must not allow the enemy of distraction to steel our focus. God has given you a plan and idea to accomplish in your life time. If you need directions on how to go about it, seek God for directions and he'll guide you. I am reminded of Proverbs 16:3 (ESV): Commit your work to the Lord and your plans will be established." Queens, God wants us to be establish the things that he has called us to. I speak into your life: you shall not be distracted, but you shall go forth in your vision and in your goals, in Jesus' name.

Your Thoughts _____

_____

_____

_____

_____

_____

_____

_____

_____

Today's Affirmation
I am going forth in the things God has ordained me to do.

Day Twenty-One
True Inner Beauty is an Everlasting Light that Never Goes Dim

Beauty Queens, I congratulate you for reaching day twenty-one; you made it! Do you realize that God has placed an everlasting light on the inside of you? Do you know what that light is? I want you to ponder on that. I want you to understand that you were born with a purpose and a plan. You are more than the makeup or the fancy hair extensions you think make you significant. We were born with a natural beauty that radiates from us since the time of birth. It's not something that has to be conjured up; it has to be unlocked from within. This beauty penetrates deep in the soul, defining the very essence of your existence.

This beauty was here before the foundation of the earth. This beauty cannot be bought with a price; it's free and made available to everyone who seeks for it. What is beauty? Beauty is the core image of God. He sent his Son, Jesus Christ, to die for you, so that you might have everlasting life, and not being entangled with the worry or false burden that this world has placed on you. I am here to tell you be free to live again. Allow the very essence of God to shine through you. In doing this, you will tap into the very person you were created to be. I speak victory into your life. May the very presence of God invade your life like never before!

I pray that the love of God finds you. Know that you are more than just breast and hips. You are Beauty Queens, the very essence of God's creation. You are called to do great things. Know that you are more than conquerors; you can do anything that you put your mind to. I want you to know that you were created with a great purpose. Some of you may have been lied to. Or you have been told you can't make it or that you will never amount to anything. I am here to decree that you shall make it. You are the righteousness of God. Ladies walk in your beauty. This is your beauty coach MandyFresh Frederic advising you to be beautiful, be blessed, and be courageous.

Your Thoughts _____

_____

_____

_____

_____

_____

_____

_____

_____

_____

_____

_____

_____

_____

_____

_____

_____

_____

_____

_____

_____

Today's Affirmation

I am God's beauty queen, full of life, and I walk in purpose.

About the Author

Mandy Fresh Frederic is a woman of faith born in Miami, FL and raised in Ft. Lauderdale, Florida. MandyFresh obtained her bachelor's degree in Business Management Supervision, and is a certified beauty expert, licensed with the state of Florida, specializing in hair and makeup.

MandyFresh is the CEO and founder of Faces Made Beautiful LLC, and operates her business under Painting Florida Pretty with Mandy, as well as Discover the Beauty Women Empowerment Organization. Her desire is to help girls and women pursue their purpose with passion. Mandyfresh uses her platform in the beauty industry to teach women about self-care and spiritual awareness by utilizing biblical principles.

To contact the author for speaking engagements, conferences, book tours and signings,

**Discover The Beauty
Women Empowerment Inc.
fb.me/MandyFresh.live
dtbwempowerment@gmail.com
(954)839-5339**